Can I Borrow Some Trust?

LaVetra Sullivan

Kingdom Builders Publications LLC

© 2017 LaVetra Sullivan
Kingdom Builders Publications, LLC

All rights reserved. No part of this book may be reproduced or transmitted in any form or by any means without written permission from the author.

Printed in the USA

ISBN 978-0-692-94784-5
Library of Congress Control Number 2017954122

Authored by
LaVetra Sullivan

Editors
Kingdom Builders Publications Editorial Staff
Louise James
Wanda Brown, Chief Editor

Photographer
Octavia Wilmore

Cover Design
LoMar Designs

This Book Belongs to

TABLE OF CONTENTS

ACKNOWLEDGMENTS V
PREFACE VIII
FOREWORD IX
INTRODUCTION XI
CHAPTER 1   IT WAS FALLING APART 1
CHAPTER 2   HOW DID WE GET HERE? 6
CHAPTER 3   THIS IS MY STORY 14
CHAPTER 4   DO YOU SEE WHAT I SEE? 21
CHAPTER 5   PARENTS AS TEACHERS 29
CHAPTER 6   MIDST OF THE STORM 32
CHAPTER 7   MOTHER'S DAY 41
CHAPTER 8   BURNED AGAIN 45
CHAPTER 9   ISSUES OF THE HEART 48
CHAPTER 10 IT TAKES TRUST 55
MORE ABOUT THE AUTHOR 58

ACKNOWLEDGMENTS

I give the highest honor to God, who is head of my life, for allowing me to be able to write this book. This has been a project that I have worked on for approximately ten years. We cannot do anything without God. We must put God first in everything we do, otherwise, we are subject to fail. Philippians 4:13 states, "I can do all things through Christ who strengthens me." Christ is my strength, my healer, and my redeemer. With the help of God, I have been able to fulfill my dreams.

I thank my mother, Mamie Anderson Kershaw, for encouraging me over the years to complete this project. She constantly asked me when I was going to finish writing my book, and encouraged me not to give up. That let me know that she supported me and believed in me. I have seen the strength of my mother as she survived many challenges in her own life. There's a saying, "No one knows what goes on behind closed doors." That's true to a certain extent. Behind the closed doors of our home, I had a mother who taught her children to pray in season and out of season. Our mother taught us to pray without ceasing. It does not matter what the outcome may be, but we must continuously pray to God to increase our strength.

My daughters, Diamond and Emerald, have been through the storm with me and have been my rocks.

My daughters have encouraged me to move forward with this book. They are truly miracles from God, and I thank God for them.

I thank my sisters, Octavia and Adella, along with their husbands, George, and Jackie, for their constant encouragement. They have stood by me throughout the years.

I would like to thank Adella for her monetary contributions to this process along with the proofreading sessions. Thanks to Minister AB Free for attending these proofreading sessions as well. I could not have done it without you guys.

Thanks to Tonya Davis, Jakeem Williford, and Tara King for the monetary contributions to the publication of this book. I would like to thank Shanika Cooper, Terese Patterson, Michelle Stokes-Glover, Scott and Jamie Stephens, Victoria Blacks, Alvin Fersner, Dawn Gressette, Minister Adrienne Johnson, Tracy Watson, Christopher Kershaw and Stephan Yearwood for constant encouragement and support.

Special thanks to Fredrecker, Tyeshia and Kaywan Shaw for all your love and support, Minister Sherrie Lewis and Marion Cobb for the countless nights of prayer. You are truly prayer warriors, and I pray that God continues to bless you.

Thanks to my nieces and nephews for supporting me through this process. All of my family, friends, coworkers, and church family have inspired me, in some way, to pursue my dreams, and I appreciate each and every one of you.

God is the maker and creator of the universe. Anyone who does not believe in God has not seen His awesome works and amazing power. God has performed many miracles in my life.

I pray that anyone who reads this book will receive a blessing from God. Know that trust is something we cannot really borrow, but something we must claim as heirs to the Kingdom of God.

PREFACE

My goal is to help those considering marriage to really think about why he or she is getting married. Marriage should not be based on how much money someone makes, or how he or she looks, or what a person can do for you. Marriage is an institution created by God, therefore, one should consult the word of God before entering into a relationship that is not His will.

I hope this book will help break the chains that the enemy holds over us as we trust that God will do what He says He is going to do. It may not come to pass the way we expect, but in the end, we will come out victorious. We may lose family members, friends, money, houses, and even trust, but in the end, God will restore us just as He did Job. We will come out stronger, wiser, and much better.

FOREWORD

When my sister, LaVetra informed me she wanted me to write the foreward for her book, I thought, "I don't feel like writing anything. Besides, she's the writer, not me. I don't even like to write!" However, I realized by her wanting and telling me to do this meant she had grown into emotional and spiritual healing, and truly she had borrowed some trust.

After her divorce, she and her two daughters lived with my family for three years. It was then that I saw how broken and untrusting she was. It was something we were all unprepared for, but because of God, we adjusted. During the course of my sister's stay, the situation was hectic and intense at times because we all had to give up something and learn to share things we hadn't before. Personally, I grew even more trusting of God. I trusted that in spite of going from a household of five to eight, our household would be peaceful. I trusted that God would provide. It didn't matter how many people said they would not allow a sister or brother to move in their homes.

I remember being told by my mother when I was a child, "Trust no man any further than you can throw him." Of course, she trusted people, but the point was to guard your heart and be watchful. The Bible clearly tells us to put all our trust in God.

This book gives insight to how some people live behind closed doors and manage to maintain in the eyes of the public. Survival is only because of God's good grace and mercy. After reading this book, I'm sure it will inspire and encourage others, as well as promote healing to many.

Remember, trusting is vital to growth. I'm happy to say that my sister has grown into trust.

Adella Elmore

INTRODUCTION

Blood dripped everywhere. I could barely hear my cell phone ring because I had entered into a deep sleep. "Who could be calling this time of night?" I asked myself. I looked out the window and saw my husband sitting in his truck, so I attempted to go back to sleep, but the phone rang again. This time I answered, "Hello," in a sleepy whisper. On the other end, I could hear my husband's best friend say, "Check on your husband." "Yeah, yeah," I replied as I yawned and crawled back into bed. "I checked on him, now good night." I hung up the phone. I became very irritated as the phone rang again. "Yes! What is it?" The person on the other end said, "You need to go outside and check on your husband." "Okay!" I said. I looked for my robe, bedroom slippers, and a coat because it was nearly twenty degrees outside. I began to talk to God.

"Lord, why do I have to go out here and check on this man who just threatened my life and our oldest daughter's life just a few days ago?" I had been searching for divorce attorneys because I was taught never to take a threat lightly. When someone looks at you with anger and rage and says, "I'll kill you," you are overcome by fear. Checking on my drunk husband was the last thing I wanted to do. I had prayed the entire week. "Lord, I can't take it anymore. Oh God, something has to change. Cover him with your blood!"

I walked out the front door into the cold night's air. As I approached the truck, my husband looked straight. I stood there for about thirty seconds trying to figure out what I was checking. It was dark. After a few seconds, I saw a stream of blood rolling down my husband's face. "What the hell? What is this?" I said. He said nothing. I grabbed my phone and called his friend back. He answered immediately. I yelled, "What is going on? Who did this?" He replied, "That's why I told you to check on him. You know how he runs his mouth. We were at the club and he got into it with Joe, and Joe stabbed him." "What was this about? I'm calling the cops." I retorted. His friend said, "He owed Joe some money for a job they were working on; one thing led to another, and Joe stabbed him." I dialed 911 as I convinced my husband to go to the emergency room. With slurred speech, he said, "Nah, I'll be fine." The ambulance came, and the EMT strapped him down to a board so that he was not able to move his neck. They wanted to ensure that he did not become paralyzed.

Even though I was angry about the week's incidents, I knew that I had to do what I had to do. The girls were asleep. I attempted to call my mother-in-law several times, but she did not answer. When she answered, she agreed to meet me at the hospital. His aunt agreed to come to the house to watch the girls.

I called my neighbor, who was my good friend, to come drive me to the hospital. My mother-in-law was not happy about this because she felt I was putting people in our business. My nerves were torn from the sight of blood and trying to clean the blood from the shower once he got out of it.

Once we arrived at the emergency room, we entered the trauma unit. Patients were being hauled in on stretchers from what were considered more serious injuries. I prayed, "Dear God, I asked that you cover him with your blood, not his blood."

The doctor came in and cleaned the wound and started him on antibiotics. I just knew this would be the end of his drinking and smoking as the knife had just missed his jugular gland, the gland that controls the taste buds. Unfortunately, the next day he was back to smoking, and not long after, drinking as well.

The number nine represents finality. The year 2009 was the year that all hell seemed to break loose. It was the end of our marriage, yet it was only the beginning!

IT WAS FALLING APART
Chapter One

Why does it seem as if bad things happen in the middle of the night? It was another late night that I was deep in sleep. My cell phone rang. I looked at the number and saw that it was my mother-in-law. Even though my husband was not at home with me, I was not afraid. I had become accustomed to being home alone with my two daughters. I answered the phone. His mother proceeded to tell me that my husband had been arrested. I said, "Okay, I'm sorry to hear that. There's nothing I can do." After hanging up, I thought, "Why did he call her? He didn't call me." We had gotten through the stabbing and now we were experiencing another setback. It was a Friday night. I went back to sleep. The next morning, I woke up and went along with my normal Saturday routine of cooking, cleaning, and doing laundry. I figured he was safe since he was locked up. Around noon he came through the door and said the judge allowed him to go on his own recognizance. He was fined a little over six hundred dollars for driving with an opened container. For the sake of onlookers and marital pride, I put a pretty bow on a damaged box. Wanting things to not look as if they were falling apart, I paid one hundred dollars a month for the next four to five months to help him keep his license and stay out of jail.

When I thought the storm was over, the winds began to stir just a few months later. My husband was sitting on the porch while the girls and I sat in the living room. I believe we had just finished supper. I could hear the truck fly into the yard. The person jumped out of the truck and began to yell, "I want my money! Where is my money?" The guy was a friend of the family. My husband had done some heating and air conditioning work for this guy who was building a new house. My husband sat on the porch drinking a beer as he acted obliviously to what was going on.

I opened the door and asked what was going on. My husband said, "Go back in the house." I responded, "No! This is my house, and I have a right to know what's going on!" The guy continued to yell, "Your husband owes me money! I gave him twenty-five hundred dollars, and he still has not finished my heating and air! I'm going to kill him!" I stood paralyzed like Sally from "Clueless in Seattle." I had no knowledge we had earned money to complete a heating and air job. So, when the truck pulled up and the sprawling began, I opened the door in fear for what this guy was going to do to my family, but when he saw my face, I became the mercy seat. In his rage, he gave my spouse fourteen days to have his money, or he would pay in court. All this time I kept asking, "When are you going to finish this job? It should not take this long." I did not know what to say or do. My husband continued to tell me to go back into the house. I went inside and called his mother. This was the only thing I knew to do. Within ten minutes she was at our house but was unable to get any answers. Instead, he cursed her out and told her she had nothing to do with what went on in his house.

Things were getting insanely ugly in the household. The arguing became more frequent and my husband grew meaner each day. I reached out to a friend of mine and she enlightened me on the signs to look for. I began to cry out to God. I said, "Lord, increase my senses!" Be careful what you ask for because God will do it. The smells became so strong. There were odors that I had never smelled before. One day I walked to the window where my husband parked his truck. I looked out and noticed that he was smoking, using some sort of pipe. It was then that I made up in my mind that I was not going to continue living this way. I knew this was not the environment I wanted for me and my children. My husband was not contributing to the household and his behavior was becoming increasingly aggressive. I insisted that we seek counsel. He agreed and we met with the pastor and his wife. After one session, the pastor and his wife concluded that we had both hurt each other badly. The session was so intense that I left in tears. The pastor and his wife were both shocked, as they had seen sides of us that they had never seen before. Because I taught Sunday School and Children's

Church and helped with the youth department and praise dance ministry, they had no idea I carried such a big stick. My husband and I went toe to toe in the pastor's study.

The weeks went by and I continued to pray. One Sunday afternoon after church I had taken a nap. When I woke up, my daughter informed me that my husband had gone into my pocketbook and used my cell phone. He did not own a cell phone, and we did not have a house phone. When I asked him about using the cell phone he said, "Yes." I told him that it was common courtesy to ask. He did not feel he should have to ask me to use my cell phone. This led to an intense argument. I heard my oldest daughter yell, "Mama!" As I turned to answer her call, I felt something hit my face as he yelled, "I hate you!" When I looked to see what hit me, I saw a tube of hair gel on the floor. The tube was light, but the force behind it was that of a brick. I went into the bathroom and applied a cold cloth to my face as there was a light bruise. As I stood looking in the mirror, my husband stood in the doorway panting like a raging bull. I said nothing as the panting continued. There was no way out. I prayed, "Lord if you get me out of here, I won't look back." He calmed down and walked out of the house. I called the police and spent the night with my girls in a hotel. The next day, I went to family court and got a restraining order. This was the day my husband and I separated.

This was the first and last time my husband threw something at me. There is no excuse for physical abuse. It is my belief that if he hits you once, he will hit you again. Don't allow yourself to be anyone's punching bag. You deserve better.

I knew this was the end of many years of emotional and verbal abuse that would begin to manifest itself physically. All my hopes and dreams were flushed down the drain.

My husband had said more than once that when our oldest daughter turned eighteen, he was going to leave. She was twelve years old at this point. We would not endure another six years of misery.

Things had fallen apart, but I knew it was time to move on. I could not look back, or I may have turned into a pillar of salt.

HOW DID WE GET HERE?
Chapter Two

I was raised in a Christian home where we were made to attend Sunday School and church every Sunday. My mother instilled in us "The Lord's Prayer" and "Psalm 23." This prayer and psalm became the scriptures that provided me with solace during the turmoil that I faced throughout my life.

Even though my parents did not always see eye-to-eye, one thing they agreed on was to instill in their four children that marriage is an institution created by God. They agreed in raising us in the fear and admonition of the Lord. My father was a trustee and musician in the church, and my mother was the youth choir director and a member of many different church auxiliaries. As children, we attended church every Sunday with our parents. In the Southern Baptist Church, it was tradition to claim a row as your family's seat. Every Sunday, we sat in the second row on the left side of the church. That way, when our father turned around from playing the organ, he could look directly at us. My mother could see us perfectly from where she sat on the choir.

Not only was a Christian education a requirement throughout our family's history, but completing high school was mandatory. We were told that we would attend college and that we had no other option. I do not say this to brag or boast, but to tell you of the standards to which we were held. Because of this teaching, when I got to college, I knew that I would meet my husband. The first guy I laid eyes on was the guy I claimed as my boyfriend. My father died when I was nineteen years old; therefore, the talks that fathers have with their daughters did not take place. Things that he probably would have stood firm on, I thought I could decide for myself. My family tried to guide me, but with my father gone, I thought I was grown enough to make my own choices.

It was not long after entering college, I saw the guy that would become my husband. I saw a light-skinned guy with low cut wavy hair and a humorous personality. We clicked immediately! We became two peas in a pod. When you saw one, you saw the other. We were a famous couple at school, and we planned for our future. I fell in love with him because he agreed that we would wait until marriage to have sex. Waiting for you and waiting with you are two different things. While he waited for me, he sowed his royal oats elsewhere. I became the laughing stock of the college campus because I was not giving it up, but my boyfriend was doing his thing.

Once he grew tired of partying and decided he wanted to calm down, he transferred to a technical school in his hometown. He promised this was an effort to save our relationship. I must say that these were probably the better years of our relationship. I continued going to school, and he seemed more focused on getting his life together. He visited me at school and home whenever he got a chance. Our relationship was reasonably strong during this time. However, we did not look past where we were.

I forgave him for all the heartache he put me through, or at least I thought I did. I took all the heartache and pain into the marriage. I felt he owed it to me to make me happy because he had broken my heart. Marriage was supposed to fix it.

When I graduated from college, I did not pray for a marriage that would glorify God and reflect His image. My options were to return home and live by the house rules of my mother or get married so that I could be independent. What an ironic twist. How do you enter marriage to gain freedom? Entering a marriage but living independently is not God's will for us. Genesis 2:24 says, "A man and woman become one flesh when they are married."15

So, a couple should come together as one, however, marriage cannot work if each person has his or her own agenda.

Before entering marriage, take the time to know God's purpose for marriage according to the Holy Bible. We can listen to the opinions of man, but we must know God's original design for marriage and build a foundation on His word. This does not mean that there will not be trials and tribulations; however, the Bible will give us the substance to withstand any obstacle that comes our way.

Anxious to marry, I said, "I do." It's every girl's dream to marry. She dreams of the day that she will hold her prince charming's hand and ride off into the sunset. I tried to get as close as I could to that dream. I rode through town in a carriage pulled by the most beautiful beige horse. The wedding was beautiful, but I had not thought a day past the ceremony. I had planned a wedding, but I had not planned my future.

Do we really stop to think about what we are saying, "I do?" You just said, "I do" to huge bills you are getting from the florist, the musician, and the minister, not to mention the owner of that horse drawn carriage! The point I'm making is that we have lavish ceremonies without focusing on the marriage itself.

Have you taken the time to ask yourself why you are getting married? You may think this sounds crazy, but trust me, I've heard it all. The older generation's hair would probably stand up on their heads, but couples do actually get married for green cards, finances, or just downright fraud. These may be quite extreme; however, there are some less extreme reasons why couples marry as well.

Even though these reasons may not seem serious, they are not necessarily for the right reasons. Some couples marry at a very young age. More teens are marrying because they think they are in love, they are introduced to sex at a young age, or to escape their parent's rules. There's the military man who marries so that he will not be alone or the pastor who marries for purity. Then there is the couple who marries because they have a child. Even though some of these marriages last, some are formed for the wrong reasons.

I have seen some of the following situations with my own eyes:

- A high school senior married a young man who had just entered the military because he could make more money.

- A man who vowed that he would not marry a woman of the same ethnic group because they had hurt him badly.

- A young lady who marries her husband because she says they are having sex anyway; therefore, they should get married.

- A young widower who has three children and needs someone to help him raise his children.

- A young woman becomes pregnant and decides she does not want to have a child out of wedlock.

- A young man sees a very ambitious young lady who has an inheritance and marries her because she is established.

Now I'm not saying that all of these marriages fail; however, I have seen the misery that some of the couples have endured. We can avoid these hardships if we take the time to consider the reasons we enter marriage.

Not only must we consider the reasons for marriage, marriage should be built on a sure foundation. One thing that my marriage lacked was a solid foundation. God revealed to me that the first thing needed in a relationship is a solid foundation. I said, "Okay God. What does a solid foundation include?" The word I heard was "trust." When you get ready to build a foundation, you take inventory of what you have and what is needed. I said, "Oh God, I don't have anything. My trust funds are empty." As God continued to show me, I realized that I was empty. Not only was my marriage lacking trust in God, I was negative in the trust area. Now I'm praying, "Lord, where do I get trust? Where does my trust come from?" When you build a house, you go to the bank to get a loan. However, when it comes to borrowing trust, there's no building for you to go. I started saying, "Somebody let me have some trust. Can I borrow some trust?" God said, "You first have to trust me." Now keep in mind this is not the only thing needed, but God was showing me one of the main ingredients. I think about how my parents had the driveway of our home paved. The cement mixture had to be mixed exactly right with the right consistency. The right amount of water had to be poured or the cement would get too hard too fast. I thought about trust being that mixture. I felt an emptiness in my stomach because I didn't even know where to start.

As I studied, God revealed to me an area that contributed to the failure of my marriage and an area that I have to work on before I can enter another relationship. The main area that I must work on is trust. I can meet someone and not trust them based on the month they were born, or the type of clothing they wear. I recognize this as unhealthy, which is my reason for writing this book. My desire is to help others who lack trust which hinders them from moving forward. I can enter another relationship, but this time it has to be done God's way. This time I will have to seek God's face and know that He is leading me into a relationship.

I constantly tell myself, "I refuse to go through the hurt and pain that another man may cause." It's difficult to let down your walls when you don't know what a person is capable of doing. Trusting is hard to do when you lack trust. The smallest look or stare that someone gives seems to cause insecurity. Your immediate thought is, "What did I do to him or her?" Your mind begins to roam. "She is mad. Why did he look at me that way?" You begin to think of your conversation or interaction with a particular person and try to figure out what you could have possibly done. You soon realize that maybe the expression had nothing to do with you. After a while, it seems as if the enemy is playing tricks with your mind. A lack of trust is actually a trick of the enemy. We must fight to take back what he has stolen from us. Doesn't it make sense that the enemy wants to steal your joy and happiness? God wants us to walk in boldness, trusting that he has our backs. If we walk around looking over our shoulders because we don't know what's coming behind us, we will definitely hit the brick wall that's right in front of us.

Trust cannot be developed over night, but with time and patience, we can build relationships that stand the test of time.

THIS IS MY STORY
Chapter Three

As I walked in on a conversation of a lady saying, "When I got shot," my mouth dropped. I felt so small. I felt the size of a pea. I said, "Lord, here I am trying to tell my story, and this lady has gotten shot!" There are so many people out there who have gone through so much more than I have and I have so much to be thankful for. God is so good in His grace and mercy. After telling her story about how she had gotten shot saving her daughter from her daughter's boyfriend, she left.

The next morning on the way to work, I began to talk to God. I said, "Lord, I thought I was through with this book. What more am I supposed to do?" God began to speak to me by saying, "You have not tapped into your full potential. There is so much more for you to tell." This was when I said, "But God, I didn't get shot! I don't have a story to tell like the lady who got shot." He said, "It's not the story, but the way it's told. No one can tell your story like you." I said, "Where do I start? What do I say?" God said, "Start from the beginning and go to the end. There are so many people out there who can be helped if they hear your story. How are they going to know what to avoid if you leave out the details?

How will they learn how to trust me, if you don't tell them how?"

I didn't feel there was much to tell about the beginning part of my life. However, you will find that many of our beliefs and ideas are developed in the early stages of our lives.

I grew up in a small town named Kingstree, South Carolina. When people ask, "Where are you from?" I say, "I'm originally from Kingstree, South Carolina." This is often confused with King Street in Charleston, South Carolina. Kingstree is the county seat of Williamsburg County with a population of approximately 3500. My earliest memory would be that of attending day care at the age of four. We drove a long blue station wagon; the kind from the tv show "The Brady Bunch." My dad was a teacher at the high school in Kingstree, so he and my oldest sister would pick me up from day care. My oldest sister is ten years older than I am. At the time, she was a freshman in high school. I vaguely remember us getting into an accident in the old blue station wagon which caused us to purchase a brand new gray station wagon very similar to the blue one. I remember taking bunny rabbits for "Show and Tell" to that same day care that I later worked as a teenager.

After day care, I attended the primary school which was named in honor of my grandfather. He was the principal of the high school, and the primary school was later named after him. My mom was a teacher at this primary school which was located directly in front of our house. It was convenient to get up in the mornings and go to school right across the street. My memories of the early years include sleeping mats and lunchboxes. This was the time before all children were allowed to receive free lunch. There were three categories: free, reduced, or full price for lunch. Guess which category I fell into. That's right; full price! Both of my parents were teachers, so according to the government, they made too much money for their children to receive free or reduced lunch. That meant we had to pay seventy-five cents a day in order to eat school lunch or take our own lunch to school. Children who brought lunch to school seemed to be ostracized. How ironic? You were made fun of because your parents made too much money for you to receive free lunch. If you didn't pay the seventy-five cents, you stuck out like a sore thumb because then it looked as if you could not afford school lunch by bringing a Strawberry Shortcake lunchbox with a bologna or ham sandwich, chips or cookies, Kool-Aid or an off brand soda. It's amazing how children are teased for things they have no control over.

We were a well-known and prominent family in the community. We were not rich, but we were successful according to the standards of the day. We had a nice house, two educated and working parents, two vehicles, and two dogs.

We were brought up under very strict rules and regulations. Children of the nineties to present don't have a clue as to what it means to live under the rules and discipline we encountered. We simply could not do what we wanted to do.

From primary school, I moved to elementary school. In the mornings we gathered in the gymnasium until the first bell rang. If the principal said, "Do not talk," that's exactly what he meant. One morning I decided to test the waters. Gathered with a group of my friends, I decided to talk. The principal, who was a white male, called me to his office. I was so afraid I almost wet my pants. All I could think about was the news of me getting a spanking getting back to my parents. If they had found out, I would have definitely gotten a beating once I got home. For an entire day, I sat with one butt cheek hanging out of the chair because it hurt so badly from the paddle. Yes, we were raised on corporal punishment. It only took that one time for me to realize not to talk in the gymnasium before school. There was no amount of bracing you could do to prepare for the hard board coming down on your behind. I don't know what kind of wood they made those paddles out of, but it felt like a whole tree fell on my butt! I learned a valuable lesson about talking when told not to. We had very strict teachers during our elementary and junior high years. Those were the days of chalkboards and recess that lasted for a very long time.

Even though we played and had so much fun, academics were the most important part of the day. I discovered my ability to write in junior high school when I was awarded for making a high score on a state writing assessment. The only extracurricular activity I participated in at the time was cheerleading. When I found out I could write, I took off with it during my high school years. I signed up for journalism all four years of high school and was a part of the yearbook staff. I entered every writing and oratorical contest my teachers presented to me. I won a number of contests which increased my love for putting words together on paper. Even though I had a love for writing, the gift was not opened until later in life.

During my eleventh grade year of high school, I entered a Black History Writing Contest with the local newspaper. I went home and told my father that I was entering the contest and that it required at least three people to qualify. I recruited two other girls from my journalism class to help me write the article. Other contest participants wrote about Dr. Martin Luther King Jr., Harriet Tubman, Thurgood Marshall, etc. My father suggested his father, William Anderson Sr. My grandfather was the second principal of Tomlinson High School in Kingstree, SC. Many may wonder why that is so important. This was during the early nineteen hundreds when segregation was still legal. Tomlinson High School was designed so that

African-Americans could receive an education in Williamsburg County. There is much history that dates back to the late eighteen hundreds concerning the origin of the school. I later learned that my grandmother, my father's mother, also taught at this school under the leadership of my grandfather. Prior to my grandfather's service, the school was held in houses located in the community. During his years as principal, the building for Tomlinson High School was constructed. It was named a Rosenwald School because funds were paid through the South Carolina Department of Education to construct the first building. A two-story red brick building which consisted of nine classrooms, an administrative office, and a library was built 1923-1924. Because of the success of the school and the increasing enrollment, the W.M. Anderson Primary School was opened in 1954. My grandfather served as principal there from 1961-1962 before he retired.

This legacy produced a family of teachers including my parents, my brother, my sister, and me. I kicked and screamed and ran from teaching for a period of time until I could not run anymore. I realized teaching is in my blood and is one of the many callings God has on my life. Because of my love for writing, teaching others to write was what I wanted to do.

I earned a Bachelor's of Arts in English and a minor in mass communications from Francis Marion University in Florence, South Carolina. Seven years later I obtained my teaching certificate in secondary English. In 2005, I received a Master's degree in Literacy from Lesley University, Cambridge, Massachusetts. It is my desire to reach and touch as many lives as I can through writing. My love for writing has now become a reality. I began to put words on paper to create the story of my life.

DO YOU SEE WHAT I SEE?
Chapter Four

It has been spoken to me more than once that I was supposed to write a book. A few years ago, I was at a prayer session standing with my arms folded and a man, who didn't know me from a can of paint, hit me on the head with a Bible and said, "Unfold your arms! Why haven't you written that book?" I was speechless. I couldn't say anything. For the past ten years, I struggled with what I was supposed to write. After my divorce, I thought I was supposed to write about the divorce, but nothing ever seemed complete. I went through periods of wanting to tell my story from beginning to end, but got depressed and stopped writing. I didn't want to keep writing about events that occurred throughout my marriage, so I definitely didn't think anyone wanted to hear about them.

Marriage is supposed to be exciting, a gift created by God. However, for fourteen years I felt as if I lived a prison sentence. I did not realize how unhappy I was until my marriage was nearly over. I did everything I thought a wife was supposed to do. I went to work, came home every day, took care of the kids, cooked, cleaned, attended church, and did all the other things a wife is supposed to do.

Being an excellent husband or wife does not make a perfect marriage. We take ideas from TV or movies and follow them and believe we are doing things the right way. After we say, "I do," we ride off into the sunset and then wake up with a person we don't even know. We return to our cozy homes and perform duties we think we are supposed to perform. We wake up, fix breakfast, kiss each other goodbye, and then repeat the cycle over again. However, there is something missing. What's missing? A number of things are missing, but the most important thing is God. I know this is not true for all marriages, but many marriages are lacking God as the center. If God is not the center of a marriage, it is very difficult to sustain.

I have studied and read so many books about marriage and relationships that I feel I should have earned a degree in this area. People enter marriages and relationships for many reasons and sometimes the wrong reasons. You often hear people say the person you marry is the person you are supposed to be with no matter what. Maybe they didn't marry the wrong person. I am not an advocate of divorce, and it is not a matter to be taken lightly. However, I do believe that sometimes we enter situations we have no business entering. Many times we focus on the end result without going through the process of making relationships work. This does not only include marital relationships but all relationships.

My parents were married for approximately thirty years before the death of my father. I watched my parents go through the ups and downs of marriage. I learned a silent lesson of enduring the heartaches and pain no matter what. I thought you were supposed to remain in a marriage "until death do you part." Who came up with that? Is that biblical? That statement almost became a reality for me as my ex-husband could have taken my life. My life flashed before my eyes as he held me hostage with his anger in a bathroom with no way out. Even though I believe in marriage, I knew that it was time for me to leave an abusive situation.

Marrying at the age of twenty-two, I did not think about any of this. I wanted to get married because I thought it was the next step after graduating from college. This is a tradition or idea that is passed down from generation to generation. Because our parents, grandparents, and great-grandparents married at a young age, we think it's the law to follow in their footsteps.

As I stated earlier, we enter into marital agreements without considering who or what God has for us. During my college years, I lost several friends because of my relationship with my ex-husband who was then my fiancé. I did not take heed when one of his partners told me I should not be bothered with him. A friend of mine from high school told me if I continued talking to my fiancé, she could no longer be my friend. At the time, I could not understand, but after many years of hardship and pain, I understood what she was trying to tell me. We often think we can be a person's hero, but we can't. Entering a marriage thinking you can change your spouse is not effective. It simply does not work.

When we look at the book of Genesis, we see that God made man in His own image. He then formed and fashioned the woman from the man's rib. The definition of form is to shape and structure. This shows us that God has the power to shape someone. We do not have that capability. I wondered why God would take the woman from the man's rib as opposed to some other part of the body. Why not his heart? Why didn't God create Eve from dust like he did Adam? When God created the animals, he did not create one animal from the other, so why was the woman created from man?

Genesis 2:21-23

21 "So the LORD God caused a deep sleep to fall upon the man, and he slept; then He took one of his ribs and closed up the flesh at that place. 22 The LORD God fashioned into a woman the rib which He had taken from the man, and brought her to the man. 23 The man said, "This is now bone of my bones, And flesh of my flesh; She shall be called Woman, Because she was taken out of Man..."

God created the woman from the man so that she could help the man. I've never seen a female animal walking along with a male animal communicating and assisting him the way a woman does with a man.

If God took a rib from the man that means that something was now missing. The woman was created to be that missing part.

The more I meditated on this, the more interesting this concept became. When someone is looking for a vital organ, they are sometimes placed on a waiting list. He or she has to wait for a suitable donor. Why don't we wait for a suitable mate? We fail to trust God to send us a person or match that is suited for us. Instead, we select someone God has not selected for us, and it just doesn't work.

Marriage is a union formed by God. If that's the case, God should be at the center. You may say, "I know God, and my spouse knows God." This may be true, but are the two of you on the same page? Do you serve the same God – the one and only true God? Are you and your spouse equally yoked? When God created Eve, he gave her everything she needed for Adam. Do you have everything that's needed to work beside your spouse? If so, how do you know? I can tell you that love is not enough. Do you have what it takes when your spouse says he or she wants to go back to school or change career paths? What if he or she decides to spend your savings on some great cause without your knowledge? These are questions that we do not think about when we are blinded by love. When we fall in love like Romeo and Juliet, we sentence ourselves to our own deaths.

As you continue reading my story, you will find that I was one of those people who married without consulting God. I didn't even think to ask God if my spouse was the person He had for me. I graduated from college on one Saturday and got married the next Saturday. My family told me that I needed to wait because I was too young, but I did not want to listen to them. I've been telling myself I will never marry again. However, I don't know what God has planned for my life. Many men have approached and tried to get close to me, but I was not ready for a relationship. One reason was that I had not healed from my marriage.

We must begin to take marriage seriously and see it as covenant relationship with God. A covenant is a binding agreement or compact. A contract is an agreement as well, but it is based on fulfilling conditions or terms. Covenant agreement is a spiritual contract with God. We don't sign any papers, we don't pay any money, and it's not based on our credit history. When you sign a contract, you make an agreement based on what the other party says he or she will do. When that party does not hold up his or her end of the bargain, he or she has broken the contract. You may then exercise your rights under the law. However, covenant says, "I'll love you in spite of, and there is no fine print."

There is no way of knowing what lies on the other side of that contract. We must make a decision to believe that our partner is going to hold up his or her end of the bargain. Trusting is hard to do, however, I believe God has a plan for each of our lives.

II Corinthians 5:7

"We must walk by faith and not by sight."

It is our responsibility to know where we are going and to whom we are yoked. After my divorce, I had to leave the place I had lived for fourteen years and move in with my family. This happens to many people after divorce, but you must know that it is okay. We sometimes have the tendency to want to turn back to that familiar place, but we must leave unhealthy situations in order to receive God's best for our lives.

I believe there were times when it was hard for me to trust because some of the things I trusted God for never came to pass. That's not to say I don't trust God. Don't make any mistake. I do trust God, but I think I learned to believe whatever will be, will be.

I remember my mother asking me after my father died if I believed he would come out of the coma. I said, "Yes, I did." At age nineteen I believed my father would come out of a thirty-day coma after having a cancerous tumor removed from his brain. Years later, I remember crying out at the altar for God to heal my brother. He had done it before, and I felt he would do it again. After my brother died, I began to think that whatever God wanted for us was going to be. This mindset became one that held me in bondage in an unsuccessful marriage, poverty, and fear.

Trust is not a tangible object that we can see with the human eye. It is something that we hold in our hearts. It makes us who we are. When others can't see the things we see, we walk by faith, knowing that God will bring us through and safely lead us to the other side.

PARENTS AS TEACHERS
Chapter Five

Our parents are our first teachers. Most of what we are made of comes from them. My sisters watched the same two people, but we sometimes have different opinions on the type of relationship our parents had. They both were born shortly after our parents married. They had a chance to witness some of the loving, honeymoon years that couples have. My brother and I, on the other hand, caught the years in which the passion seems to subside or grow dormant. We watched our parents argue and watched tolerance turn to bitterness, which turned to plain old tiredness. No one was happy, but no one was sad because everyone figured life was something to live, so just get through it. My sisters decided that they would not tolerate the challenges my mother endured. I, on the other hand, viewed these challenges as a way of life. My marriage was almost the epitome of my mother's, however, the consequences of my poor choices did not allow mine to last as long as hers.

Even though my father drank, taking care of his family was the top priority. We always had a roof over our heads, food on the table, and lights to see.

On the other hand, my ex-husband did not seem to care if the lights were cut off because in his childhood he had gone without lights. He felt as if it was no big deal if the lights were cut off. I went years without a house phone after struggling to pay that bill and keep a cell phone at the same time. I commuted forty-five minutes to work and had small children, so I felt a cell phone was necessary, so, I opted to give up the house phone. This was just one of the many sacrifices I made for my family to have food and a roof over our heads.

Endurance had become my middle name. It was the longest fourteen years of my life. My first test of endurance was not long after marriage. The first stages of marriage are when you have to make the tough decisions. It's then that you have to decide what you are going to tolerate. If you don't decide then, you may as well not fuss about it later. This is when you learn the person, or should I say ugly monster, that you are with. You may ask, "Well, don't you know all of this before you get married?" A person can hide what he or she wants for a very long time. However, when you begin to live with that person on a daily basis, you begin to see the good, the bad, and the ugly.

We hadn't been married six months when my husband got fired from his job. He was working on a construction site at his mother's job. He came home upset saying that he was falsely accused of catcalling. Even though this was the 1990's, this behavior was not tolerated, especially if you were accused by the white race. Being the supportive wife, I consulted our family's attorney, who informed us that nothing could be done. When you work a job without a contract, the employer has a right to fire you without giving you a reason.

During the first stages of marriage, I had to decide if my spouse was right or wrong, or if it even mattered? Am I going to allow this type of behavior to continue? The answer was, "You have to find a job."

It did not take him long to find a job. He landed a good job with a local heating and air company. Things were going well, or so I thought. After about two years of steady employment, my husband came home and said he had been laid off. It was months later that I found out he was not laid off, but got fired because he tested positive during a random drug test. In spite of what the paper said, he stuck to his statement that he was innocent.

As children, we learn to tolerate unhealthy behaviors based on what our parents have endured. We watch their struggles and think it is okay for us to suffer the same ordeals. Unfortunately, we continue to live under a curse that only we can decide to break.

MIDST OF THE STORM
Chapter Six

Trust is not only an issue when it comes to marriage. A lack of trust spills over into other areas of our lives such as our jobs, health, and our finances. I woke up one morning and God instructed me to write. That week I had been stressed out over bills and how they were going to get paid. I was living pay check to pay check for years. Correction! Not even pay check to pay check, but having more month left than money. When you are broke and frustrated sometimes writing or even talking is the last thing you want to do. Your mind constantly races trying to figure out what you can do.

Many authors write books after they have overcome, but God was instructing me to write in the midst of the storm. So, here I am, not even sure where my next meal would come from or if I would have enough gas to get to work on Monday, and God was saying, "Write!"

After a week of trying to figure out who or where I could borrow money, God said, "I don't need you to borrow any money; I need you to borrow some trust!" Tye Tribbett's song, "*Same God*" kept playing in my head. God was reminding me that if he did it before, he could do it again. He took me back approximately nine years. I was married at the time, and my ex-husband would work off and on. That means he would get a job and would not keep it, or he would work side jobs as he called them. Side jobs were jobs that paid him under the table. He made cash money as soon as he finished the job, but it may have only been enough for him to put gas in his truck to get to the next side job.

He said that he wanted to own his own business, so he experimented with working on his own. Well, this was not a good experiment for him. He would say that he was putting in bids for jobs and that he was going to get a major heating and air contract. I supported him in every endeavor or business adventure that he tried to make. We had gone all year, and our house was already set to be auctioned during the tax sale. There's a certain amount of time that is given before you can redeem the property. A friend of mine called to let me know she had seen our names in the newspaper. I said, "Thanks! I know." This was an everyday conversation as I asked my husband what we were going to do. He would come home every day from supposedly working and sit on the front porch and smoke and drink and say, "Oh I didn't get paid like I was supposed to this week." There was always a story.

Did I say that I was making the house payment each month not to mention paying every bill in the house?

Things had gotten to be too much for me to handle; therefore, I let the house phone go and used my cell phone as my main phone. Because things were so tight, I didn't even have enough to keep minutes on my cell phone at the time. I had had enough! I made up my mind that if the house had to be auctioned off, so be it!

I went to work one day as usual and looked up at my door and saw my sister. My family had been trying to call me and could not get me because the phone was off. She came to my classroom and said, "What's going on?" Mama said, "She's been trying to call you and your phone is not on." That's when I had to come clean and let them know that we were struggling and about to lose our house. Yes, I said, "House, not home." We needed twenty-five hundred dollars within a few days or we would be on the streets. I figured the girls and I could find an apartment, and I really didn't care where he ended up. When my sister and my mother found out, they pulled together with what I came up with, and we paid the property taxes. I debated whether or not to tell my husband we had the money because he was a user and taker. He kept saying he was going to have a thousand dollars, but as soon as the taxes were paid, that went away. I kept telling him I needed the thousand dollars so I could give something back to my mother and sister, but sadly, I never saw the thousand dollars, and neither did he. I asked God, "Why did this come back up?" He said, "I needed to remind you of how great I am. I am the Alpha and Omega, the beginning and the end. I am Jehovah Jireh, your provider."

Even though I eventually ended up letting the house go, it was very difficult. I always considered it sentimental because my brother left money for my husband and me to get a house after he passed. We lived with my husband's parents for five years. Six months after we got married, we were already having financial problems. I was determined to prove everyone wrong that said we should not have gotten married so soon. Why couldn't we make it? There were couples that had gotten married and did not go to college who had successful marriages. I thought because I obtained a college degree, that I would get a job easily. Those were my thoughts, but no one had taught me reality. I was determined to make it, so I worked two jobs. With the two jobs that I had and the job my husband had, we still could not make ends meet. We had no savings. We moved in with his mother and stepfather which was a huge mistake. I am thankful that I had a roof over my head, but it was like being in prison for five years. My brother died during this time and left money for us to get out on our own. I felt obligated to do everything in my power to keep the house. This could have worked except I didn't know the enemy was living under the same roof. He did everything in his power to fight against this. Instead of being appreciative, he said that he didn't want the money that was given. He would have rather worked for his own money to build us a home. My mother paid fifteen thousand dollars in cash from the money my brother left to purchase the land that we bought. This is why it was so hard for me to let go. My brother and I were really close. I felt like I owed it to him and my family to do everything I could to save our house. In the end, I realized that a house made of sticks was not worth my health and sanity neither that of our children.

There were many times I was covered by God's grace. My ex had gotten a construction job with a man who had gotten a number of contracts and who had been in the business for a while. He convinced the business owner that he was the man for the job. He had gotten fired from jobs, but when a business owner wants to cut corners, he will overlook things that would normally disqualify an employee. My ex had a way of convincing people to do what he wanted. He persuaded the owner to write him a check for eight hundred dollars in advance. I didn't know the details, so I followed along. We were broke, so an eight hundred dollar check was much needed. He told me that we had to go to the bank where the check was written in order to cash the check. The bank was approximately one hour away from where we lived. We drove there and cashed the check and then went to the store. We needed a number of things, so we went shopping. We bought boots, clothing, groceries, and items for the children all totaling approximately two hundred dollars. This left him with six hundred dollars to buy the supplies he was supposed to purchase for the job. The next week the owner called my ex-husband because he was not supposed to cash the check at that time. After I heard the profane language through the phone, I realized that he was not supposed to spend any of the money on himself. Once again I had trusted my husband's every word. This was one of the many situations that continued to cause the cord in our marriage to be broken. It does not matter what kind of challenges we face in marriage or life, we must put our trust in God and not man.

According to CNBC, finances are the leading cause of stress in a relationship (CNBC.com). We were broke the day we got married. What little money we had was spent paying the remainder of the bills from such a beautiful wedding. My last dollars were spent on my fairy tale ride with horse and buggy to live a life of happily ever after. I just knew it would all fall into place. I thought, " Who needs a savings account or money when you have true love? We would work together right?" Columbia, South Carolina was my Harlem. I would relocate and find my dream job and make lots of money. Within the first few weeks of marriage, I took a hostess job at a local restaurant. That would help out until I found something else. I found a job at an insurance agency working as a clerical worker. I held these two jobs at the same time until I tried selling cars at a dealership. After two unsuccessful months, the manager agreed to let me host and direct customers to salespersons to buy cars.

After approximately six months, I finally found a job that I liked and that could pay some of the bills; however, we had already moved in with my in-laws. The plan was to save money, get on our feet, and then find a place of our own. A six month goal turned into five years. I worked as a supervisor for an inventory company. I made good money, but the hours were long and unpredictable. My day sometimes started at 5:00 am and could last anywhere from four to eighteen hours. I worked for this company for two years and some months until I became pregnant. I knew that I would not be able to continue working long shifts with a new born baby. I had to find something more stable, so I worked temporarily at an insurance company again as a clerical worker. I then began to realize that none of the jobs that I had were promising. I knew that I was supposed to work with children, but did not know where to start. I had enrolled my baby in daycare, so why not start there? I taught four year-olds for two years and began researching the process to gain my certification as a public school teacher. I taught first and second graders at a private school for one year until I finally made my way into the public school system.

This was not the end of this long journey. I began this adventure as a substitute teacher. I applied with different school districts. One day I received a call from a district that was approximately fifty miles from where I lived. One of the English teachers had to stop work immediately because of health issues. This was my chance to get my foot in the door. I took it! I commuted fifty miles one way for two years, then that dreadful day came when the bad news of budget cuts. All first and second year teachers were given letters of termination in the district I was working. I thank God for favor. Before the ink could dry good on the letter, I was hired in a nearby district. I completed the certification process, received my master's degree, and gave birth to my second child during this time.

Philippians 4:13
I can do all things through Christ who strengthens me.

If you trust and believe in God, you can do anything. This is when our faith and belief is exercised the most. Sometimes we find ourselves in the midst of the storm, but we must remember that God is there with us.

MOTHER'S DAY
Chapter Seven

While there are many effects of divorce, depression and anxiety are among the few that impact your mental, physical, and spiritual health. May 11, 2014, Mother's Day, I woke up early feeling depressed. I couldn't figure out why I was feeling this way. About two years earlier, right after my divorce, my daughters and I rode with my sister and her family to our hometown to visit our mother. I got up that morning and washed my hair. I decided that I would go natural and let my hair air dry. As an African-American female, there needs to be a little more maintenance when it comes to wearing natural hairstyles. I thought that I would just pull my hair back, and it would remain crimpy once it dried. Unfortunately, I was wrong. Once we reached our destination, it looked as if I had stuck my finger in an electrical socket. We got to my mother's house and everyone gave their hugs and kisses, but I sat on the couch paralyzed. Tears began to flow like a river. I had no control and did not know why I was crying. Research shows that tears are one of the most powerful forms of healing because they release toxins from the body. I could not talk or move. I could only cry and feel the pain bottled inside of me.

I finally gathered enough strength to go out to eat with my family. We went to a local restaurant, and everyone ordered their food, but I headed to the restroom. I was experiencing a full-blown anxiety attack. Anyone who has had anxiety knows the symptoms. I could not eat anything that day. When we got back home, I went to bed and slept it off.

Two years later, I was traveling to my mother's house again. This time I was much healthier and stronger, but when I woke up that morning, I felt depressed. I asked God why I felt this way. I could not figure out why I wanted this day to be taken off the calendar. I thought, "Who came up with this freakin' holiday?" As I wallowed in my anger I said, "Isn't every day Mother's Day?" We work every day, all day, and someone decided that one day out of three hundred and sixty-five days, mothers should be recognized. I couldn't pinpoint from where this was coming. I knew it had nothing to do with my childhood or my mother. I tried to think if I had a bad experience with my ex-husband that would make me despise Mother's Day. I felt like Grouchy Smurf. "I hate Mother's Day," is what went through my head. I went back to sleep and decided that I did not want to go to church.

When I woke up again, the revelation came to me that I would be nothing without my daughters. I thank God for my daughters. We have struggled, but I thank God that I am their mother. To all mothers who are sometimes discouraged and wonder why we celebrate Mother's Day, know that it is a blessing to be a mother.

Eight years ago, I had a miscarriage. This is one of the most devastating experiences a woman can ever experience. God reminded me that it didn't have to be this way. Many mothers have lost children at birth or later in life. It is one of the saddest things that can happen to anyone. God said to me, "I chose you! I imparted the wisdom and knowledge in you that you need for your children. It took a Rebecca to raise an Isaac. It took a Bathsheba to raise a Solomon. It took a Hannah to raise a Samuel. It takes you to raise your children!"

Mothers should be grateful for their children. My heart goes out to women who have miscarried or lost a child at birth or even in adulthood. Before I miscarried, I had friends who had miscarried. I sympathized with them, but my God, when I experienced this for myself I was able to empathize. To think of the women who have had multiple miscarriages makes me cringe. This was truly a test as I did not realize how strong I was. I thank God for sparing my life and allowing me to be a living testimony for other women who have experienced a loss. Know that God is able to heal our bodies, emotions, and our minds. We must continuously pray that God strengthens us during these times and equips us with the weapons of warfare. This comes through reading His word along with prayer and supplication. Give every area of your life to God and he will sustain and keep you in any circumstance or challenge you may face.

BURNED AGAIN
Chapter Eight

I had decided that this was the last time I would be burned. I thought this time would be different. Another endeavor or business adventure had gone wrong. People always tell you, 'This time will be different. You must trust and believe! You must have faith!" Here I go again putting my all into something only to be disappointed. Last year I planned a summer program with a friend and her husband. I suggest this to no one! To make a long story short, my friend offered me a chance to use a building she and her husband owned. I had several meetings with her and her husband to organize the program. The day before the program, her husband called me and said, "I'm going to pull the plug on the program." I was crushed. However, at the last minute, God secured a building for me to run the summer program. Even though things did not go the way I wanted, I made it through and broke even in the end. Here I am a year later wondering how I got myself into another mess. All I could hear was, "You have to trust! You must have faith." So that's what I did. I worked a different camp diligently and faithfully only to be cheated again. I asked God, "Is it me? Why do people keep doing this to me?" I had been burned again. I don't think it hurt as bad that particular time because it was in the same spot. When you are burned in the same spot, you become immune and you don't feel the pain as much.

I asked God why he would have me include this section in this book. God revealed that at one point in my life I put more trust in a man than I put in Him. Sometime before I got married, I went to visit my ex-husband who was my fiancé at the time. I lived in one town, and he lived in another about an hour and a half away. Two young adults in love, the distance didn't seem much. So, there I was, a young fool in love. Blinded by love, I thought my fiancé had my best interest at heart. He wanted to take me around and show me off to his friends. We rode in my car to his friends' houses. There was one stop we made that I wasn't too sure about. As we walked in what was called a shotgun house, I latched on to his arm. I trembled as we walked through the house and he called looking for one of his friends. I asked, "Why are people lying on the floor?" I grew up in a stable home, therefore, I had no knowledge of crack houses. I gently pushed him and tried to convince him to get me out of there because I was terrified. From there we went back to his mother's apartment. She asked about our day and what we did. I told her about the visit to the crack house and she said, "He took you there?" By her facial expression, I knew that she was not pleased and that she knew the dangers of that place. Why didn't this open my eyes?

It didn't because I stood on his every word and trusted this man when I should have been focused on God. I didn't tell any of my family members or friends because I knew they would have killed me. I thought to myself, "Oh, I can't judge him because of his friends. He's not on crack, so it will be okay." I thank God for keeping me through my ignorance. What interest would a young man have in a crack house? That's food for thought.

We must trust God instead of putting our trust in man. When we put our trust in man, we expect things to go the way we want. Trusting man leads us blindly into places we never thought we would end up. Thank God for covering us when we "*walk through the valley of the shadow of death.*" The enemy wants to destroy us, so he leaves out the details. However, God brings us out victoriously and "*prepares a table before us in the presence of our enemies.*" We come out anointed and appointed to do the work of God. (Quotes from Psalm 23)

ISSUES OF THE HEART
Chapter Nine

I conducted a workshop entitled "Issues of the Heart" for young girls ages thirteen to nineteen. There were six speakers who spoke on the topics of unforgiveness, hurt, emotional abuse, self-esteem, healing, and the power of human touch. My topic was unforgiveness. My daughter spoke about emotional abuse and how it has impacted our lives. The things that my ex-husband, her father, said to her, caused damage in ways that cannot be seen with the human eye. There were feelings that she expressed that I was not previously aware of.

The presenters shared personal stories and ways to overcome unforgiveness, hurt, and pain. The next day, two young ladies contacted me and poured out their hearts. I asked God, "How can a father walk around and act as if he does not have children? What gives him the right? How can a mother curse her daughter and call her names that cut so deep?" We wonder why people walk around and hold hurt in their hearts toward the ones who are supposed to love them but have damaged them.

That next night I had a dream. My ex-husband was in a vehicle with his mother and his aunt. They were sitting waiting as we prepared to go on a family vacation. When I awoke, I was reminded of the many times that we traveled and invited his family. He and I never traveled as an item. He made sure that accommodations were made for his family. It did not matter how I got there because he was going to stick with his people. My brother died in 2001. When I got the news, I began to cry. I went to my husband expecting to be consoled, but the hug was not heartfelt at all. The next morning, I packed clothes for the baby and me and headed home. He did not take off work or try to go with me to my family's home. He came down the day of the funeral with his family and stayed the night and we returned home the next day. There were many occasions that I was left alone to go through, but this one sticks out the most.

Another incident that I can remember happened in 2007. People wonder how you can be so mad at a person to the point that you don't want anything to do with him or her. When a person leaves you to fight on your own or turns his or her back on you, you feel betrayed. At this time, I found out I was pregnant. This would have been our third child; however, I miscarried. I started having strong contractions. Getting my husband to do anything responsible was not in the picture. I told him I needed to go to the emergency room. He began to drink more than he already had that day. We gathered our two daughters and took them to his parents' house which was less than two miles away. Once we dropped them off, he drove around curves like a bat out of hell. I was not sure what was going on at the time. I started screaming, "Slow down. You're going to cause me to lose the baby!" He started cussing, and I realized the more I talked, the crazier he was going to act. I just started praying, "Lord help me!" When we arrived at the hospital, the emergency room was packed. I sat waiting, crying in pain. There was a man beside me whose blood sugar level was over 400. The receptionist was coming around asking the urgency and telling people they were backed up because there was a trauma. I asked her if there was any way I could go to the maternity ward. She said that if I had been at least four months they would have taken me. I sat for hours until finally, they took me to a room. I was bleeding heavily, and the pain was excruciating. The doctor came in and said, "You may be miscarrying, and it could be a matter of life or death." The doctor would not tell me that I was definitely miscarrying. I remember looking up at the T.V. in the room watching Joyce Myers. I began to pray, "No weapon formed against me shall prosper!" After the doctor examined me, he sent me home. There was an older nurse who told me at least three times, "Get to your OBGYN!" By the time we left the hospital, it was around 7:00 am. We went straight to the OBGYN.

Once again, the doctor examined me, and I continued to bleed. I was sent home where I bled for days and finally saw the remains of what would have been life. Not only had I carried a baby that did not come to life, I delivered unforgiveness that lied dormant in my womb. Unforgiveness manifested itself in a way an army takes out its adversary. It affects our bodies in ways we do not realize.

Unforgiveness is a poison. It is when you hold a grudge against someone or something. Some people are still holding grudges from childhood. Some have held on for years and years and do not even know why. Until recently, I was one of those people. I held on to things because I felt if someone wronged me, he or she should pay. The way I made them pay was to cut them off. About two months ago, I saw a lady I know in the parking lot of a local grocery store. She shared with me that her sister had passed two weeks prior. I offered my condolences. She went on to share that her sister died mad at her over an unresolved issue. That encounter was a divine appointment. She did not have to share this with me, but for some reason she did. One, because she was hurt, and two, because God meant for me to hear it. God had been dealing with me for some time about unforgiveness. When I heard this, I made up my mind that I was not going to continue to hold on to things that people have done to me. Was I tried? Yes! Am I still being tried? You best believe I am!

Situations came up in which I would normally get frustrated and say, "Well, I'm not going to deal with that person anymore. I'm not putting up with it!" The enemy would say, "But, look at how many times this person has done this to you. So, you're just going to let it go?" It was hard to let go because that's what I was used to. I had to keep telling myself, "Let it go!"

Unforgiveness not only starts out small, it starts when we are small. We nurse her and keep her close to our hearts. We don't let go because she reminds us of what has happened. When someone comes along to help us out we say, "Umm, No! This is mine! You don't know what I've been through. I'm not giving her up!" People on the outside see what we are doing is not healthy, but we don't see it that way. Unforgiveness is weighing us down. They offer help, but we get ugly with them. "Why are you worrying about me?" At this point, unforgiveness has grown and is almost as big as you are. You begin to look overwhelmed, and it's showing in your face. She's getting heavier and heavier, and eventually, she becomes bigger than you. She is so big that people can no longer see the real you. She blocks you, and you begin hiding behind her. When people speak to you, unforgiveness takes over and portrays herself as you. You are in the back screaming, but nothing's coming out because she has silenced your real voice.

This is what unforgiveness did when I was stuck in a bad marriage. This is what unforgiveness did to my children. We had to learn to walk in forgiveness. That doesn't mean that you allow people to treat you anyway, but when they do, you can say, "It's okay." When you walk in forgiveness, you don't see things as if someone is always trying to set you up. After my divorce, I told myself that I would never allow another man to hurt me the way my ex-husband did. When I say hurt, I'm not talking physical abuse. It hurts when someone calls you the b word. It hurts when someone tells you that you are just supposed to be quiet and have babies. It hurts when an alcoholic stands over you and threatens to kill you and then wants you to lie down with him. Unforgiveness sits on you and lowers your self-esteem to make you think you must do something you do not want to do. Unforgiveness weakens you and places fear in your heart.

You may ask yourself how could this be? It is because the first thing the enemy attacks is your mind. He plays with your mind! He tells you things like if you want to measure up, this is what you will do, or you wouldn't want people to know that things aren't perfect in your world, or that you don't have it all together. This comes from not forgiving others in your past or not forgiving you from placing high expectations on yourself. You have expectations that you must live like the next person; however, when you fail, you become mad at yourself, God, and the entire world. You must forgive yourself for coveting what others have. You must ask God for forgiveness for not consulting him in the first place, and then you must forgive others for things they have done to help create the monster in you.

IT TAKES TRUST
Chapter Ten

Once I decided to try dating, God revealed to me that every man is not my ex-husband. I did not realize I was making other men pay for the wrongs of my ex-husband. I considered everything a lie, and my motto was, "Guilty until proven innocent." After being hurt so many times, you don't believe anything people tell you. Hurt and pain will cause you to imagine things that are not even real. You create scenarios in your head and over process situations. I knew that my thinking was unhealthy, but this did not stop me from thinking that way. God reminded me that things take time and that I must be patient in finding the right man. Trust is something that has to be practiced. You may ask how in the world can you practice trust? When situations arise in which you lack trust, you have to remove all of the negativity and tell yourself to trust God. When you trust God, He will instruct you in the things you need to do.

I am now in a place I never thought I would be. Six years passed in which I felt like I had been traveling through the wilderness. I seemed to be going around in circles and not making any progress. All of a sudden, I got to a point that seemed hard to move forward because I did not know what was ahead. I'm sure many of you have experienced wanting to stay in the wilderness because it seemed like a safe place. You search for something new and exciting, but because you have been waiting so long you begin to doubt and are afraid. You know what you are looking for, but you don't believe that it will ever come.

In the wilderness, you walk by the same people day in and day out. You think no one will ever walk into the wilderness to show you another land. You know no one wants to be there; therefore, you don't expect anyone to come in. You are only trying to get out.

There are soft spots in my yard. When it rains, the land gets muddy. If I continue to park my car in the same spot, the holes only get worse. In order for that spot to heal, I must park somewhere else. We can't look for someone who is right beside us in the wilderness. That person has the same mindset and mentality. The wilderness causes you to hide because it is a place you do not want to exist, and you don't want others to know that you are there.

I learned a valuable lesson from my twenty-year-old nephew. As children, we grew up along with members of the opposite sex. We were close and did not think anything about becoming romantic with our male friends. We played together on the playground, we fought and made up, and didn't think twice about it. We didn't hold long drawn out discussions as to why we were mad. We just knew the argument was over and that we were still friends.

My nephew has a female friend who he calls his sister. His mother and I insisted that he liked the young lady and that she liked him and they just weren't aware. He explained that they did at one time, but they both agreed to remain friends. In the beginning, I could not understand that concept. The Lord continued to reveal to me that relationships don't have to start out romantically. It's like putting the icing on a cake that hasn't been baked. I imagine that would be some heavy stuff. With the icing being thicker than the batter, it would drop to the bottom, creating a terrible mess.

Throughout my fourteen years of marriage, my ex-husband made me think that sex was love. Because of this, I felt that a man could not possibly be interested in me unless he wanted to sleep with me, so I concluded that no one could love me for me.

I am learning to take down my walls and trust that relationships can be built from the ground up. The Lord continued to reveal Proverbs 18:22 to me which states, "The man who finds a wife finds a good thing." He showed me that the man who seeks me out will be looking for a good thing; not a good time.

MORE ABOUT THE AUTHOR

LaVetra Sullivan - 1973 Resided in Kingstree, South Carolina. A 1991 graduate of Kingstree Senior High; in 1995 earned a Bachelor of Arts degree in English with a minor in Mass Communications from Francis Marion University in Florence, SC; in 2005, earned a Master's degree from Lesley University, Cambridge, Massachusetts.

Sullivan coordinated many school and community projects over the past twenty years. She began her teaching career in the private sector and moved to public education in 2001 with her first teaching assignment at Edisto High School in Cordova, South Carolina.

In 2003, she started working with Calhoun County High School in St. Matthews, South Carolina, where she is currently still employed. She was Teacher of the Year, Freshman Academy Lead Teacher, After School Homework Center Coordinator, and advisor for various clubs and organizations. Ms. Sullivan has taught ninth through twelfth grade English for the past sixteen years and has been selected to take on a new role as English Department Chairperson. She also teaches Reading, Journalism, and African-American Literature.

LaVetra has spearheaded and worked summer and year-long projects throughout Calhoun and Orangeburg counties which include a tutoring and writing business entitled Enrichment-on-the-Go, Girls in Pink, an organization for girls ages 13-18, and Angels of Praise, a praise dance team. She is a member of The Pen of a Ready Writer Society, an organization for aspiring writers in Columbia, SC.

Her hobbies include reading, writing, and acting. She acted and performed in many church and school plays as a child and won several oratorical contests throughout high school and college. Her most recent performance was in the stage play "Lord, Please Help My Family" written and directed by Pastor Raymond Brown.

LaVetra has worked for the past two years to fulfill her lifelong dream of becoming a published writer and author with her first publication entitled *Can I Borrow Some Trust?* This book about her journey before and after marriage will touch the lives of many as they weigh the advantages and disadvantages of marrying at a young age. She hopes to teach others to pray before making life changing decisions. She has shared most of this journey with her two beautiful daughters Diamond and Emerald Sullivan from a fourteen-year marriage. She and her daughters currently reside in Orangeburg, South Carolina and attend Cornerstone Community Church in Orangeburg, South Carolina.

Her goals in life include continuing her studies and making an impact on society through her writing. She would one day like to own a home for at risk girls who may be confused or transitioning in life. Her favorite scripture is **Jeremiah 29:11**, "*I know the plans I have for you. Plans to prosper and not fail. To give you a future and hope.*"

www.ingramcontent.com/pod-product-compliance
Lightning Source LLC
Chambersburg PA
CBHW042051290426
44110CB00001B/29